HAZEL: THE OUTLAW MUMMY

4/16/21

BOB DEMOSS

Hey Tom, Here's that short story I was telling you about. Enjoy the ride!

Bob

Copyright ©2021 Bob DeMoss.
All rights reserved.
Published by DeMoss Publishing Group, LLC.

No portion of this book may be reproduced, stored in a retrieval system, or transmitted in any form or by any means—electronic, mechanical, photocopy, recording, or other—except for brief quotations in printed reviews, without the prior permission of the publisher.

Cover design by Thom Schupp.
Cover copyright ©2021 Bob DeMoss.

Printed in the United States of America

CONTENTS

Chapter 1	1
Chapter 2	12
Chapter 3	21
Chapter 4	29
Afterword	35
Also by Bob DeMoss	41

CHAPTER ONE

Without a good wink-hood
A Hoodwink can't wink good
And, folks, let me tell you
There's only one circus
With wink-hooded Hoodwinks!
The Circus McGurkus!
— Dr. Seuss

The first clue that I was headed for an abnormal encounter worthy of *The Barnum & Bailey Circus* was buried in the wording of a classified ad: "Interested persons must apply in person after 6 p.m." An address without a phone number was provided. That seemed odd.

Why the secrecy?

I dismissed the thought. I had bigger issues at the moment, namely, my wife and I were moving to Nashville that weekend. We needed an apartment while we hunted for the perfect place to build a home—ideally with several acres, tall trees, and a view.

Scanning *the Tennessean* classifieds, I spotted the ad for a quaint two-bedroom house in the country. The price was right: $400 per month—almost too good to be true. The landlord also had several acres for sale on a cul-de-sac overlooking a lake and a golf course.

Best of all the location had the perfect proximity to town, and yet was remote enough to be private. The digital readout on my dashboard indicated the time was 6:15. With nothing more urgent on my plate, I figured I'd give this spot a shot.

I pointed my candy apple red Miata convertible toward Franklin. Fifteen minutes later, I turned down a pea gravel road, stopping at the first house on the right. The mid-August sun was starting to dip below the wooded hillsides as I surveyed my surroundings.

The neighborhood appeared to be a collection of houses built in the seventies sitting on oversized lots lining both sides of a dead-end street. The landscape was punctuated with several dilapidated barns, relics from years gone by, much like what I saw back in Pennsylvania where I grew up.

As I got out of my car, a gaunt-looking, charcoal-brown bovine with discolored ivory horns lifted her head. I'm no cattle expert, but she looked closer to becoming beef jerky than a spry youth. Not the kind of cow you'd feature in a *Got Milk?* commercial.

She studied me with a long, sad face from behind a barbed wire fence. A soft, lazy breeze drifted through the tall grass where she stood alone. The place felt peaceful, if somewhat neglected—sort of like the pathetic cow.

I checked the address on my paper and, not finding any street numbers, approached the nearest house—a brick ranch style home. A heavyset woman wearing a dirty, floral print dress, appeared at the screen door before I rang the doorbell.

Four youngsters, who all looked to be under the age of ten, scurried forward from within. They huddled around her skirt, anxious to see who was calling. With a brush of her hand, she shooed them away.

I introduced myself and asked if I were at the right address. As I spoke, her eyes widened, perhaps with a touch of alarm.

"Oh, you're looking for Luther's place," she said. She bit the left corner of her bottom lip.

"I am?"

A nod. "Yes, he's over there. Two houses up the road," she said with a jab of her thumb and a tight smile as if something had soured in her mouth. "His house is on the left, the one just beyond Battle and those two wretched bulldozers he keeps in the yard."

"Battle?"

"Luther's cow."

I leaned to the left to see where she had pointed, noticing the somewhat rusted John Deer dozers for the first time.

"Thanks," I said, turning to leave with the strange feeling as if I had somehow offended her. "Hope I didn't bother you —or the kids."

She hesitated. "You do know he's a . . . *difficult* man, right?"

"Can't say I do. Never met him."

"Well, then." She flattened her skirt with nervous hands and, with a labored turn, started to retreat into her house. She paused, pivoting to face me. "You might wanna hurry. You don't wanna show up after dark."

"How's that?"

Her forefinger tucked a loose strand of hair behind an ear. "It's really not my place to say . . . but since you look like a nice enough fella . . ."

"Thank you, ma'am."

"I'm not trying to alarm you," her eyes narrowed, "But, he might just shoot you—and ask questions later, that's all."

I laughed. "Is that so?"

She forced a thin smile.

I figured she was just pulling my leg. And yet, I found myself wrestling with the feeling that I should hop in my car and find an apartment complex managed by someone who didn't own a shotgun.

"Listen. It's none of my business," she said interrupting my thoughts. "Luther is, well, an *unusual* fellow. The last guy who rented from him lasted only a couple of months."

"Lasted?"

She stole a glance in the direction of Luther's house. When her eyes met mine, they searched my face as if she were trying to warn me off without saying as much. She lowered her voice a notch. "Look, I've already said enough."

With that, she vanished into the darkness of her house and closed the door.

Puzzled by her peculiar behavior, I made my way back to the Miata sensing I was being watched as I reached for the car door.

I looked up and, while I'm not entirely positive, thought I saw the curious woman peering through the window blinds in my direction. I smiled and waved and then slipped behind the wheel. I inserted the key in the ignition, and then stopped.

Why was my heart starting to race?

What did she mean by *lasted*?

Convinced my imagination was getting the better of me, I cranked the engine and eased the car up the road. As I passed by the grassy field, Battle stopped chewing mid-munch; I slowed for a closer look at the Brahman cow, admittedly a curious sight for a guy born in New Jersey where Holstein's don't have horns.

Battle stood as motionless as a living fossil. Several

seconds later, her tail whipped a fly off of her backside . . . or, was she, too, waving me off? Dismissing the thought, anxious to get to the potentially trigger-happy Luther before the sunset, I pressed on.

A mahogany brown, split-rail fence outlined the perimeter of what looked like six acres of land. I couldn't help but notice a dilapidated wishing well, decorative not functional. The well was what you might see on a mini-golf course. Homemade, definitely not store bought.

Someone had snapped the thing together from brown aggregate cement posts and tacked woods slats on the roof, although much of the wood was rotten or missing.

The traffic jam of thick wisteria vines and tall grass, sprouting here and there, were sure to choke any wish from ever being granted.

Moments later I rolled to a stop at the bottom of Luther's driveway, parked, and left the keys in the ignition for a faster getaway if needed. I grabbed my cellphone, texted my wife so she knew where to find me—just in case things got weird.

I got out of the car and headed toward a man wearing jeans and a short-sleeve blue shirt, Luther, I presumed. He stood at the top of the driveway near the three-car garage. His back was to me and he didn't turn around as I approached.

To his right, a small mountain of freshly cut firewood, probably three cords' worth, was piled along a stone wall. A rusted, fifty-gallon water tank lay on its side adjacent to the wood. Three, maybe four, gas cans of various sizes, a log splitter, and two chainsaws littered the driveway as if he were preparing to have a yard sale.

The retreating sun, with its tired rays of illumination, cast a burnt orange glow on the late afternoon visit. The middle of the three garage doors just beyond Luther was open.

While I couldn't quite see inside without the aid of additional light, it was clear that Luther had a collection of more stuff in various heaps, piles, and bins than a south Philly junkyard.

I was about to call out his name when, almost sensing my presence, the man turned and looked in my direction. He appeared harmless enough, that is, until I noticed he was clutching an object in his right hand.

A gun, perhaps?

Closing the distance between us I discerned he was holding an ax.

Make that a bloodied ax.

That was a first for me. I inhaled a sharp breath. I reminded myself this was Tennessee country—snake handlers, high-octane whiskey made in backyard stills, hard living and all of that hick stuff, right?

After all, where I came from in Colorado, meeting a guy with a bloodied ax happens less often than, say, a visit from Halley's comet. Makes a guy wonder where that blade had last been used, you know?

For all I knew, this guy had a private abattoir in his basement. He could have been like one of the psychos you read about in the papers—the kind of guy who has a freezer full of body parts. Was this what the old woman was trying to warn me about?

Temporarily losing my voice, my eyes drifted to the ax.

While I'm no detective and have no training in forensics, I was fairly positive that the blood wasn't fresh . . . recent, but not fresh. The sticky, reddish brown fluid, like chocolate syrup on ice cream, coated the edge of the blade in drips.

And, while Luther bore a strong resemblance to Ted Bundy or Jeffery Dahmer, I was pretty sure Bundy and Dahmer were still pushing up daisies in a cemetery for their crimes against humanity.

I studied Luther's hands with short glances so not to

arouse the suspicion that I was scrutinizing him. His mitt-sized hands, for that they were—leathery, tanned to the color of my old Wilson baseball glove, appeared vice-like.

An indent formed between his first and second finger where he pinched the filtered end of a cigarette. His skin had a yellowish-red cast, like someone who had spent too much time in a tanning bed, or maybe from a heavy application of *Tan in a Can* spray.

Luther took a final pull from his cigarette, flicked the toasted filter to the ground where it tumbled into a weathered collection of discarded butts.

In that moment, I felt as if I were standing in the presence of the Marlboro Man.

Tall. Lean. Seasoned like a hundred-year-old oak tree. A manly man. A throwback to the kind of guy who, like John Wayne, could survive with his bare hands, a knife, a knapsack, a good horse, and a tin of beef jerky.

"Well, you're look-in' some kinda pretty, Momma Kitty," Luther said, addressing a calico cat with beautiful markings weaving in and around his feet.

Having scampered out from under a nearby bush, she arched her back against the cuff of Luther's pant leg, purring. Luther reached down and offered a quick scratch, then added, "Looks like we got ourselves a real city slicker."

Not exactly sure how to take his comment, I stepped closer and extended my hand.

"I'm Bob. You must be Luther."

Luther straightened up. He towered at least a foot over me. He had to be all of 6'8" not including the natural straw hat perched on his head. He was clearly amused at something I must have missed.

"Well, that depends on who's asking."

A wry smile creased his face as his hand swallowed my

hand, sort of the way a snake swallows a mouse. I confess his callused grip almost crushed my milk toast fingers.

"I . . . I saw your ad for the rental property and the land for sale." I released his hold.

"That so?" Luther said. He tucked the ax under his left armpit. With a practiced hand he fished another cigarette from a pack of Vantage smokes in his front pocket and lit up.

"What'd she tell ya?"

"Excuse me?"

"Claire . . . the woman over yonder," Luther said with a nod down the street. "The big one, in the muumuu dress. She's so heavy, she could jumpstart a 747 jet."

He simultaneously coughed and laughed at his joke.

"Oh, right. Claire," I said, nodding in agreement now that I made the connection. Come to think of it, she never gave me her name.

For a second, his sea blue eyes narrowed.

"I seen y'all talking."

My face flushed. Unsure what that exchange had to do with the rental or the land, not wanting to prolong the encounter any more than was necessary, I figured at least part of the truth was the best course of action.

"She said you could be, um, *difficult*."

Luther seemed unfazed by the comment but waited for more.

"Oh, and she said you might shoot me if I came after dark."

He smiled at that, his eyes now twinkling as if the thought appealed to him.

"Well, alright then."

"Look, I'm sure you're busy. I can come back later—"

"Nah," he said, waving me off with his cigarette lodged between his fingers.

Try as I did to talk about his rental and the property for

sale, he seemed in no hurry to get down to business. He took a drag, then blew a series of perfectly formed rings of smoke.

In the course of the next ten minutes I learned Luther had built his own house, bulldozed his own ponds—four of them—in which he raised catfish the size of small dogs and, if he could be believed, was fixing to chop off the head of another rooster, thus the ax.

"I'll show you how to drain the blood and pluck his feathers," Luther offered.

"Maybe later," I said. Fishing for a plausible excuse, I added, "Can't say I'm dressed for the occasion."

Personally, I'd rather have a stick in my eye.

My idea of a good time was to get this deal done, then catch up with my wife for dinner at the Loveless Café, a country joint we had heard so much about. Frankly, I was growing more uncomfortable with every passing minute. The sun was now beyond the point of no return on the horizon, at least for the evening.

I glanced at my watch and cleared my throat.

"Luther, about the rental and the land . . . are they both still available?"

His eyes narrowed and, for a moment, felt as if they might just bore a hole through me. I got the impression he was sizing me up, his gaze now scanning me like an X-ray machine.

"They are," he said. "Follow me in here, slick."

Slick?

Before I could object, Luther turned and headed toward the house while Momma kitty scampered in the opposite direction. For a second I thought that maybe I, too, should follow her lead.

Not wanting to appear rude to my potential landlord and neighbor, I followed him into the oversized, deep and dusty garage, careful not to stumble over the clutter of tools and engine parts strewn about like tripwires.

Luther, several steps in front of me, reached toward the ceiling and, with a yank, pulled the chain dangling from the overhead exposed joists. A lone light bulb, maybe all of 60 watts, struggled to chase away the darkness. As the three-car garage came into focus, I studied the maze and variety of junk—literally everything but the kitchen sink.

The 1977 Cadillac Eldorado coupe enshrined in the left bay was difficult to miss. I paused to admire the classic. This baby was loaded with the opulent Biarritz package.

I'm talking opera windows, power everything, pillow-tufted leather seats that looked like a posh country club sofa, dual-tone hubcaps, gleaming chrome bumpers, and a grill so thick it could double as a cattle prod.

Navigating my way through the jungle of odds and ends, I came to a giant metal carcass of something about the size of a Prevost tour bus engine. Call me nosy, but I had to ask.

"Excuse me, but what's that thing for?"

He turned around, rested a hand on the machine like a trusted friend, and announced, "This right here is a genuine Heidelberg Windmill Letterpress. If ya treat her right, she'll take good care of ya."

He winked, then brushed the top of the press with the side of his hand before continuing toward the back recesses of this cave-like space.

I'm thinking, *Just what every homeowner needs*, right?

I mean, there's nothing like owning your very own printing press—all 3,000 pounds of steel, tubes and rollers. Given his love for the mechanical beast and the ax in his left hand, I kept my sarcasm in check.

I stepped over quart-sized cans of screen ink scattered across the pathway, along with reams of paper stacked in piles, probably for the next job. I couldn't figure why this country man who had several head of cattle, two bulldozers, four catfish ponds, a few dozen chickens, also needed a printing press.

When Luther's neighbor Claire told me that he was "unusual," maybe she was referring to his eclectic collection of gear and livestock.

No doubt that was part of her thinking.

The other part came into focus as my eyes adjusted to the dim lighting. Twelve feet in front of me, tucked under the stairs, was the last thing I ever expected to see in anyone's garage.

A coffin.

CHAPTER TWO

The faded gray and bluish wooden casket, parked beneath the staircase, was covered in a thick blanket of dust.

As I stood there with Luther and whatever was in that box, time slowed to a snails' pace, creeping along, leaving a trail of questions with every passing second.

Unsure about the legalities of storing a body in one's home, I studied my exit strategy and determined that the only way out was the way I had come in.

I half expected the garage door to close behind me blocking my avenue of escape.

Luther fished another cigarette from his pocket and, using the embers from the last one, lit up. Watching this man who I'd known less than twenty minutes inhale, I found myself wondering what kind of tortured soul would keep a coffin in his garage?

I once read about some wacko in California who had twenty, maybe thirty, caskets stacked in his two-bedroom house—some large, some kid-sized. Just my luck I stumbled on a guy who probably impaled little animals as a kid.

Spying the eight-foot long, white freezer chest just beyond and to the right of Luther, chilled the marrow in my bones.

As Luther shuffled toward the casket, the garage felt decidedly warmer, musty, even tomb-like. His smoking didn't help matters. I felt dizzy at the thought that maybe I had been lured into a mass murderer's lair.

On the other hand, maybe there was a simple explanation for storing human remains in a garage—if so, I just couldn't think of any. I mean, some people collect model trains, Beanie Babies, Kewpie or Barbie Dolls . . . but bodies?

Then again, maybe there wasn't a body.

Why would there be?

Maybe Luther built coffins as a hobby. For all I knew he was a craftsman who wanted to show off his work. He had built his house, so he had carpentry skills. Using scraps of wood to make caskets as a side hustle was a conceivable explanation.

Stranger things have happened, right?

For his part, Luther appeared to be enjoying the moment; he craned his neck like a vulture anticipating the death of a wounded animal.

Although I was no match for this grisly, death-obsessed, ax-carrying man, I didn't want to appear weak by revealing my fears, for that might embolden him—at least that's what I'd read somewhere.

I had to appear strong, unflappable.

The Alpha Male.

Luther bent down, moved a carburetor and a ratchet from the floor, and then rolled the casket toward us, out from under the staircase. The casket rested on a floor dolly as if it were a giant toolbox and he were some kind of hardware salesman at Sears.

In that moment, I wondered whether Luther was married.

Did he have a family?

Did he have a stash of bones around back?

Would my wife ever find out what happened to me?

Luther reached down and put his hand on the lid of the casket. Now standing inches from the coffin, I assured myself that there was no way he was going to open that thing, right?

Wrong.

Before I could squeak out a word of protest, I found myself gaping at a petite, very dead woman, about the size and height of my grandmother.

She wasn't wrapped in long strips of mummy bandages like I saw as a kid watching *The Three Stooges* episode "We Want Our Mummy." A plain white cloth draped across her waist was a nod to modesty. That's it.

Her red hair was shoulder length, as straight and ridged as the bristles of a broom. Her skin, browned with age, taut as a drum skin, pulled against her skeletal frame and vacant eye sockets. Her arms lay across her stomach and her bony fingers had long, sharp fingernails much like talons of an Eagle.

I found my voice and, thankfully, remembered to breathe.

I wanted to ask, who was she?

When and how did she die?

What if anything did Luther have to do with her death? Was this the remains of the last person who wanted to buy Luther's land?

How could he get away with storing a body in his house, anyway? And, why would this man keep her body as any sane person might collect baseball cards or antique bottle caps?

In answer to my unspoken stream of questions, Luther hiked one boot onto the edge of the casket, folded his arms and launched into a carny-like spiel much like a carnival barker:

"Step right up—see Hazel Farris," Luther said, as if working the big top.

"Gaze upon her face. Touch the leathery skin of American's only outlaw mummy. With steel nerves and deadly aim, on August 16, 1905, Hazel shot and killed five men in Kentucky, then escaped to Bessemer, Alabama where she fell in love, was betrayed to officers, and ended her own life rather than submit to arrest. Just twenty-five cents to see this genuine human mummy. Exhibited to the public for the benefit of science."

When he finished, he took a drag from his cigarette.

Me? I was still trying to dislodge my tongue from my throat.

Noticing I was speechless, Luther said, "Old Hazel and I used to make the rounds in the circus."

"She's a mannequin?" I finally managed to say.

"Son, you *are* a city slicker," he said with a laugh, punctuated with a series of coughs. "She's the real thing. She was born in 1880 and died five days before Christmas on December 20, 1906. A perfectly preserved mummy. A mystery of science. A work of art." Luther threw his head back and launched into his stage routine:

"Come one, come all. Don't miss Hazel Farris. Teeth still in her mouth, hair on her head. The exhibitors will pay $500 in cash money to anyone who examines the body of 'Hazel the Mummy' and can prove she's not the genuine article but a replica. This is a bona fide proposition, made in good faith and without reserve whatsoever. Any and all doctors are invited to examine her in a time and manner which suits their convenience."

In spite of his $500 reward, I had no intention of touching her body. Or examining her.

Or combing her hair.

"Funny story," he said, oblivious to my shock. "One night with a tent full of ticket holders, the power blew. Four portly women took out the side of the tent, my partner, *and* the ticket booth trying to escape!"

I half expected the overhead lightbulb in his garage to blink off right on cue. If so, I'm pretty sure I'd've make a hasty exit, too.

"Tell ya what, son" Luther said, plucking a vintage handbill off of a shelf. He handed me the yellowed and dog-eared promotional piece, maybe something printed on his Heidelberg. "You can come back anytime that suits your fancy. She ain't going anywhere." Another smirk.

While I'm not usually at a loss for words, this occasion was the quintessential example of being tongue-tied. I felt as confused and upside-down as Alice in Wonderland.

All I wanted was to rent a house.

Maybe buy some property.

But this guy was selling tickets to see a dead body. Seriously? I couldn't process everything myself, so how was I gonna explain all of this to my wife?

"Luther," I said after tucking the handbill into my pocket, "Hazel's great, but I'd really like to talk about your *rental*."

"You like catfish?" came the reply.

"Not sure I've ever had catfish."

"Well, you're in for a treat, old Bob," he said. "Stop by tomorrow for lunch. I'm fixin' to make a mess of catfish. We'll talk about the rental then."

I confess Luther's fried catfish was as fantastic as was the reason why he had ponds filled to the gills with the whiskered fish.

Years back, he and his wife went to a seafood joint in town—a rarity since Luther distrusted others to prepare his food. Since they weren't super hungry, they intended to split a plate of catfish.

Their request was denied by the management.

Luther was livid. He left and vowed to raise his own so he could eat as much or as little as he wanted—which struck me as a bit dramatic. Then again, everything about Luther was bright, bold and bigger than life, albeit eccentric.

Like the gold foiled wallpaper with raised red velvet swirls in his hallways, the red and black wall-to-wall shag carpet whose tufts were long enough to rake, the 20' vaulted ceiling in his great room with twin fans flanking a triple wagon wheel chandelier, and an enormous, floor to ceiling stone fireplace.

After lunch, we sat in two oversized leather recliners facing a large flatscreen TV so massive it could serve as an alternative heat source on a cold night.

A player piano rounded out the entertainment options.

Actually, scratch that.

With a *thwack*, I heard and then saw what looked like a trap door situated high upon the wall, to the left of the stone fireplace. A gray squirrel scampered down the face of the chimney as if he owned the place.

"Did you see that?!"

"Awe, that's just Wild Bill," Luther said, entertained by my astonishment. "He comes and goes as he pleases . . . a nervous little fellow, but he's alright."

As much as I wanted to ask about Hazel, there was always a sideshow going on in Luther World. "Okay, I gotta know. Where'd you run up on Wild Bill?"

"I was bulldozing over at Alan Jackson's place—"

"The country singer?"

"One and the same," Luther said, lighting up a cigarette. "Used to dozer for him and a bunch of those singers . . . Kix Brooks from Brooks & Dunn, Amy Grant, Smitty—they're all good people." He tapped the ash into an ashtray the size of a hubcap.

"Anywho, I knocked over a tree while clearing the land when this feller with a partial tail hit the ground. Just a baby, he was. I brought him home, fed and raised him. 'Course, don't see as much of him after he went into heat. Now and again he'll drop in for a visit."

"So, Luther," I interrupted. "Why did Hazel shoot her husband in the first place?"

He considered that for a second. "She wanted to buy a new hat, is all."

"Wait, what?"

"Hey, I wouldn't have pulled a stunt like that," Luther said. "Them two was known to be hard drinkers. Neighbors heard 'em yelling all the time. Can't say for certain, maybe she had too many hats already. Money could've been tight. Anywho, the extravagance enraged her husband. They exchanged harsh words. Refusing to back down, Hazel grabbed a pistol from the bureau, and shot him dead is what she done."

"Over a hat?"

I couldn't conceal my disbelief.

Luther waved me off.

"Yup. Back then *everyone* wore hats 'bout as often as we wear shoes—includin' young'uns' and old timers. Winter hats, summer hats, Easter hats—you name it, the Montgomery Ward catalogue had something to fit the occasion. Slick, those women wore hats with plumes of ornamental feathers enough to make a peacock jealous."

"Let's say I buy the hat theory. You said she shot *five* men . . ."

"That's 'cause the shooting was heard by three policemen passing outside their house. They rushed in to investigate." Luther paused for effect. "Hazel was a crack shot and didn't hesitate to fire on them intruders. All three went down, landing on her husband's lifeless body."

Luther took a swig from a can of Dr. Pepper.

"The deputy sheriff, summoned to the scene by neighbors, entered from the rear. He figured he'd take Hazel by surprise, and then overpower her. During their struggle, he stumbled over the other bodies and his revolver discharged—taking with it Hazel's right-hand ring finger. When he regained his footing and stood up, the officer received the shot which ended his earthly career."

He snuffed out his cigarette in the ashtray, stood to leave, and beckoned for me to follow him down the hall. Trailing several steps behind him, I said, "Let me guess, that's when Hazel ran for her life?"

He offered a nod—as if I had stated the obvious. He opened a door at the end of the hall to yet another large room, maybe 20' by 30' filled with a hoarder's delight of more odds and ends.

I did a quick scan of the room.

For all I knew, he had another mummy stashed somewhere in the heaps of paper and bulging boxes.

To my right, I saw a Shure SM58 cardioid microphone clipped to a chrome stand, a pair of 5' tall Peavey speaker columns—each with four 12" speakers, wired into a Peavey mixer. I used to play in a 50's style rock 'n roll band so I was familiar with the gear. I had no idea he played.

As I was trying to make sense out of this development, Luther strapped a Gibson acoustic 12-string guitar over his broad shoulders, then slipped a harmonica holder around his neck. He stepped to the microphone and, morphing into his Elvis alter ego, introduced himself as *Eldorado*.

For the next few minutes he sang several songs including an original entitled, "Just for You Dad."

I offered my sincere applause—he was quite good. After

the unexpected concert, "Eldorado" handed me a 45 recording of the tune which included country star Janie Fricke singing background vocals.

Not sure how he pulled that off.

When we returned to the living room, Luther stopped and said, "Slick, I've prayed for someone like you to come along. I'd be happy to rent ya the house."

"Thank you, Luther," I said.

We shook hands.

"Door's open. If you like the place, move in anytime y'all want."

"How do you want to handle the rent?"

He regarded that for a moment.

"Don't worry, son, I know where you live."

CHAPTER THREE

Several days after moving into the cottage Luther told me to get a gun. Nothing heavy duty, he said. "Get'cha a .22 caliber pistol from Walmart; that'd be just fine." I did, although uncertain why.

Our backyard was like a park. Tall, mature trees towered overhead providing a canopy of shade. A stream wandered along the back edge of the property. And, to complete what looked like a Norman Rockwell painting, a 100-year-old barn with a faded red tin roof, leaning to one side, sat about twenty feet from my bedroom window.

The way I figured it, Luther didn't bulldoze the barn primarily because it served two functions: it was Momma Kitty's personal playground—I'd see her darting in and out of it all day—and, he used the left side as a chicken coop and a fenced yard behind it for the hens to roam.

Inside the barn, the coop was a simple affair; ten nests on the right and four horizontal poles on the left served as perches for the chickens to roost upon at night. The place hadn't been cleaned in maybe 50 years. Maybe 100. Chicken droppings, like stalagmites, formed below the roosts.

The interior featured more milky-white spiderwebs per square foot than a haunted Halloween display at the mall. Mice darted in and out stealing whatever the chickens failed to consume during the day. And the blanket of gray dust was so thick, a battalion of Molly Maids armed with fire hoses couldn't clean the filth in a week.

This particular night, I was awakened from my sleep—the kind of sound sleep so deep it causes you to drool on the pillow. The chorus of squawking erupting from the barn was so loud it could raise the dead.

Unsure of what was provoking the commotion, I slipped into my sandals, grabbed my flashlight, a cheap plastic special, and headed into the night. As I approached the barn which, frankly, seemed taller, darker, and more ominous in the thin moonlight, my imagination jumped into overdrive.

What if a coyote was inside there attacking the hens?

Luther had said they'd been seen in these parts, even took down a horse the month before. The thought of facing a fanged predator under the cloak of darkness set off a few dozen warning bells inside my chest.

I paused and considered retreating to the security of my bed. And yet, the screeching of the helpless chickens compelled me onward.

With a groan of wood-against-wood, I slipped the makeshift wooden door lock to the left, pushed on the door to the right, and braced myself for the worse.

The 25-watt bulb suspended from the ceiling by a three-foot, tattered extension cord, offered meager light, half of which was hidden by a thick mesh of cobwebs. The pale glow of the yellowed lightbulb revealed little.

With my heart pounding and my mind racing to know why the chickens were wailing, I shoved the rickety door another few inches. Like an invisible force from within working against me, the door refused to yield further. I trained my flashlight inside the barn, searching for the cause of resistance.

Just inside the door, the beam of light caught the bloodied face of a possum making a meal out of one of the hens. I confess I was so unprepared by the encounter with Mr. Possum that I fell backward, grabbed the door and pulled it tight.

I stumbled back to the cottage to get my gun.

This wasn't KFC. The critter's chicken dinner meal plan had to be stopped.

Luther had charged me with the safety of those chickens. They needed me. I wasn't about to let this unwelcome predator go unpunished. If I did, he might look for a free refill and takedown another one of the helpless sisters.

How could I explain to Luther that several of his prized Rhode Island Reds died on my watch?

I kept the pistol on the top shelf in my closet. With hands shaking, I fumbled and eventually managed to jam six bullets into the chamber. This was showtime, although the closest thing I came to firing a gun in real life was pumping quarters into Lethal Enforcer, a video game at the mall.

Locked and loaded, I ran back to the scene of the crime, pushed the door open, and scanned the room for the intruder.

At first, I didn't see the possum. He must have been aware that he had messed with the wrong guy. I figured he probably ducked out through the little pet door-like opening, which the chickens used to come and go during happier times. If he had left, however, the chorus of squawks should have ceased. They hadn't.

I glanced at the chickens huddled together, pushing and vying for safer positions on the highest perch. On the opposite side of the spiderweb infested space, the pointy nose and beady eyes of the possum registered in my peripheral vision.

He had taken refuge in the dark recesses of the barn, hoping to remain undetected so that he could finish his grisly business. With my heart pounding in my ears, I raised my arms and pointed the gun.

The first shot missed.

Okay, I admit I was rustier than a discarded paint can sitting outside in the rain. I certainly didn't have the "steely aim" of Hazel with a pistol. I mentally regrouped, assumed my video game stance, and fired again.

BOOM!

The possum tumbled in slow motion to the floor, clearly hit between the eyes just above its pointed gray snout.

That, of course, wasn't good enough. He had to pay for his crime.

I emptied the .22 into its carcass to make sure he'd never mooch again.

Now what? I spotted a century's old shovel in the corner and decided to scoop up the dead beast. Dangling off the edge of the upturned blade, I carried the corpse outside to the stream which meandered behind the barn.

Much like the Nordic tradition of sending dead bodies adrift, I tossed Mr. Possum and his rat-like prehensile tail into Dry Branch Creek. I returned and did the same with the remains of the fallen bird.

The mood of the remaining chickens changed dramatically. They took their places on the perch, standing on one foot with the other tucked in close under their breasts to stay warm. By two a.m., with my hands washed and clothes changed, I crawled back into bed.

The next morning arrived with an unwelcome rattle outside of my bedroom window. At first the sound didn't make sense. The fog from my late-night showdown had yet to lift from my dream-induced state.

The high-pitched *putt putt putting* reminded me of George

Jetson's space-age flying car in The Jetsons—that classic Saturday morning cartoon from my childhood. With a final series of clanks and a whoosh-like exhale, the sounds stopped.

Semi-awake, I thought, *Just my luck—a spaceship has landed in the backyard.*

The silence that followed was deafening.

I was tempted to rollover and catch a few more winks, but that's when the singing started. Someone with a smooth, baritone voice, with a sprinkling of Elvis Presley's vocal technique, launched into a heartfelt rendition of "Wasn't That a Party" by The Irish Rovers:

Could have been the whiskey
Might have been the beer
How in the world
Did I end up here?
Wasn't that a party?

I leaned toward the window, pulled back a corner of the drape, and stole a look.

Luther was dismounting his old green John Deere Gator. The five-wheeled runabout sported nubby black tires and a cargo box littered with gas cans, weed eaters, gizmos and gadgets, two fishing poles and a net. I had no doubt his ax and a maybe his shotgun were tucked somewhere in there.

That's when it hit me—I had invited Luther to breakfast. He was bringing the eggs and I was providing the rest. How could I forget something like that?

I slipped out of bed careful not to wake my pregnant wife, yanked on shorts, a tee-shirt, and my sneakers, then headed for the back door. Suppressing a yawn, I said, "Hey Luther."

"Well, if it ain't old preacher Bob." Never one to miss anything, he added, "Sleeping in, was we?" He handed me a dozen brown eggs from his hens.

Another yawn. "You would've too if you had had my night."

"*Wasn't that a party*—" he riffed. He followed me inside, ducking his head so as not to hit the top of the doorframe. I opened the fridge, grabbed a few items then started laying out bacon strips in an old cast-iron frying pan.

Tapping his front left shirt pocket where he kept his Vantage cigarettes, Luther said, "Mind if I smoke?" I looked over and exchanged a smile. That was his idea of a joke—he'd smoke in his own home but never when he visited us because he knew my wife was expecting our second child.

I started cracking his brown eggs into a mixing bowl. "How about a feta cheese omelet with a side of bacon and English muffins?"

"Slick, whatever blows your hat back into the creek is fine with me."

Luther helped himself to the orange juice in the fridge and a glass from the cupboard, then sat down. While we had started to bond over the last few weeks, part of me felt the need to walk on eggshells around him. I wanted to believe him about Hazel being a notorious outlaw, but the story was so fantastical.

Admittedly, I was struggling with the truth of it. For all I knew, Hazel was some sort of made to order Mail Order Mummy. You know, a science project replica fashioned from papier-mâché. I planned to dig deeper into his backstory after breakfast.

At the moment, something didn't look right with the eggs. I need to be careful not to provoke this man whom I was still getting to know, especially since we hadn't finalized the sale of the track of land at the top of the hill.

I said, "Luther . . . nothing personal, but there might be something wrong with your eggs." I tilted the mixing bowl in his direction.

"See how these yokes are neon yellow? Are they okay to eat?"

Maybe his chickens ate toxins as they pecked for grubs in the dirt. The thought wasn't far-fetched. Several days back Luther told me how he'd bury garbage in his fields—a practice, he assured me, country folks had been doing for Centuries.

In addition to burying sick or diseased cattle that had to be put down, Luther had laid to rest his old pickup truck and a water heater which had died a few years back. Used motor oil was dumped in for good measure. A case could be made that uranium was lurking in the barnyard where the chickens roamed.

He waved off my concern. "Son, that's 'cause them eggs are fresh. And the shell's thicker, too. Those store-bought eggs city folk buy ain't worth a dime. They're old as the day is long."

He was right about the shells being stronger. Breaking them to scramble felt like trying to crack open a golf ball.

"But, what about this? There's *two* yokes in that one."

Having never seen double yokes in my eggs, I was growing convinced the mutation was a byproduct of some radioactive agent in his groundwater.

"Quick, slick!" Luther said with a wry smile, "how 'bout let's call *Ripley's Believe It Or Not.*"

I refused to take the bait. "How about *you* call 'em about *Hazel the Outlaw* . . ."

"Yup. Already did. Years ago."

I let that comment go, unsure whether I could believe *him* or not. A few minutes later I served up our Day-Glo omelets and figured a prayer of protection was in order.

"Mind saying grace for us, Luther?"

He removed his straw hat, looked heavenward with a

beatific smile, and said, "Through the lips, past the gums, lookout tummy, here it comes!"

Not exactly what I had in mind.

As we ate, I told him about the previous nights' events, feeling good about my role as Defender of the Coop killing the possum. I thought he'd be proud.

He listened to my tale with mild amusement. Pretending to take a drag on a cigarette, he said, "Son, you should've just left the carcasses alone."

"You mean, leave them rotting on the floor?"

"That's right, slick," he said, "Those chickens would have eaten both of them in the morning."

I couldn't help but think, Maybe *that's* why they laid fluorescent eggs.

Luther added, "Be glad you didn't bump the electric fence by the creek last night."

Just to be clear, I pointed through the window toward three horizontal wires draped on a series of rusty three-foot metal posts. The barrier was a relic and likely short-circuited a decade ago. "Wait, that old fencing?"

"Yes sir, that electric fence will light up the cigarettes in your pocket."

CHAPTER FOUR

With breakfast finished, we sat out back in a couple of plastic lawn chairs left behind by the previous occupant—who may or may not have been buried in the yard, perhaps inside of a pickup truck six feet under. Just saying.

Luther tapped out and lit up a fresh smoke. Momma kitty wandered over from the barn where she had no doubt feasted on a few unlucky mice. She jumped onto Luther's lap, settled in, licking her claws as if savoring the remains of her last kill.

Across the street Claire, who had cautioned me about Luther, was busy pinning clothes to a clothesline and stealing glances in our direction as she worked. I looked over at her and offered a friendly neighbor wave. She turned away, started singing something off-key, and then scampered back inside her house with an empty laundry basket.

Luther just shook his head.

"That lady sings like a Volkswagen engine trying to start on a cold winter morning."

"She's no Janie Fricke that's for sure," I said, anxious to

start asking a few questions about Hazel. I wanted to get him talking before Claire returned for an encore appearance.

"Now, Luther, don't get me wrong . . . it's not that I don't believe you about Hazel's hair and nails growing after her death. But doesn't that seem *odd* . . . and maybe a tad hard to believe?"

"Whoa! Ease back on those horses, son," he said, tossing the charred remains of his cigarette to the ground.

"My Granny Brooks, God rest her soul, would never tell a lie. *Never*—unlike those politician hoodlum types up in Washington. They're more crooked than the devil. They'll screw you, the horse you rode into town on, and the dog that followed you in!"

I'm thinking Luther was the one who needed to ease back on *his* horse.

He pressed the point: "Granny assured me she'd trim Hazel's fingernails and her long red hair going on five years, all the whilst Hazel was in her garage."

I held up my hands in surrender. "Okay, but how did she ended up with Granny and then with you almost a hundred years after she died?"

Luther puffed out a ring of smoke.

"After Hazel fled Kentucky, she fell head over heels for a man in Bessemer, Alabama, some say he was a police officer, who professed love for the lonely fugitive. She relied on his honor and integrity as a lover and, probably in a drunk-brag, confessed to the shootings."

"A guilty conscious has a way of doing that," I said.

"Yup," Luther said with a nod, adding, "That old rascal made haste to betray her to collect the $500 bounty on her head. Learning of his betrayal, refusing to be captured, Hazel killed herself December 20, 1906."

With a flick of his forefinger, he knocked a red wasp off of his forearm before continuing.

"Medical specialists and morticians who've examined her believe she drank high quantities of some sorta concoction of arsenic or poison and whiskey, which did the deadly trick. Her corpse was carted over to Adams Vermillion Furniture store which doubled as a funeral parlor selling caskets. I heard tell since Hazel was an orphan, that's why nobody lay claim to her body."

The orphan angle made sense to me. I figured back in 1880, the year Hazel was born, the practice of hospitals recording birth certificates had to be sketchy at best. No way they'd be able to find her birth parents.

Luther interrupted my thoughts. "Several months went by and nobody came 'round looking to claim her, so Adams figured he'd seize on a business opportunity. He charged thrill seekers 10 cents for a glance at his notorious guest whose body wasn't decomposing."

Luther brought his cigarette to his mouth, speaking while holding the butt with his lips.

"Right about 1907, my great-uncle Olanda Clayton Brooks caught wind of Hazel's remarkably preserved body and gave $25 cash money for her mummified remains."

"Because?"

"Son, O.C. Brooks was an old school carny working the carnival circuit—not one of those fly-by-night shysters hawking who knows what kinda gimmick. He traded in things that were *real* and *unusual*—"

"Kinda runs in the family," I said, but I don't think he heard my quip.

I glanced in the direction of his garage. If anyone was the *King of Unusual*, that'd be Luther—what, with Hazel laying mum under the stairs, Wild Bill the squirrel darting in and out of his house, albino catfish trolling the bottoms of his ponds—not to mention Battle grazing in the field and

Momma Kitty on his lap. Kinda felt like he was running his own circus.

I studied the lines on his leathered face as he stared skyward at a passing cloud. Each wrinkle and crease, no doubt, had been fashioned by a colorful past.

For a brief moment, I sensed his memories were transporting him back in time.

"See the one and only Murderous Mummy," Luther blurted out, startling Momma Kitty.

His hand punctuated the air as he announced:

"This wild, hard-drinking Kentucky woman was a terror with a gun, or a hatchet if a pistol wasn't handy. Her shrunken form, though beautiful in life, is well-preserved and on exhibit to entertain and amuse the exacting public. Saturday will positively be the last day. Don't miss this moral exhibit for the benefit of science."

Pleased with his practiced pitch, he took a pull on his smoke. "The first thing Uncle Olanda did was to park Hazel in my grandma's garage up in Nashville whilst he traveled back to Louisville to find her relatives."

"Any luck?"

"You might say so," Luther said, shooing Momma Kitty off of his lap. He stood and, with three long steps, grabbed an RC Cola from the cooler on his Gator. He popped the top, took a swig, then sat down.

"He did find some kinfolk but none of them rascals wanted to fool with her body. So, in 1911, Uncle Olanda's conscience was clear when he added Hazel to his show . . . and 18,000 people paid a nickel to see her over the first ten days."

A lawnmower roared to life on the adjacent property. With a point, Luther said, "That's old Louie the drunk. '*Have beer can—will travel*' is his motto. He's got a cold brew going already." Luther pretended to stand up, announcing, "Better get me a Bud-*weiser* . . . so I can be smart."

The joke took a moment to sink in.

"How long did your uncle travel with Hazel?"

Sitting back down, Luther said, "From about 1911 to 1943. O.C. did carnivals in 48 states. He traveled with Hazel's casket strapped to the side of his Model T."

"What if her casket fell off?"

"Yeah, that happened a time or two." Luther leaned back and stretched, then said, "He was doing so good he upgraded his wheels to one of them 1931 Oldsmobile's—a gray one. He pulled the backseat so there'd be room for Hazel. Guess how many folks paid to see her?"

I had no earthly idea. I shrugged.

"Slick . . . more than 500,000! Uncle Olanda pulled in about a million bucks. Ya might say she was one Money Making Mummy."

He smiled ear to ear.

"Wasn't he afraid someone might steal her?"

"Yup. Never let Hazel out of his sight." Luther paused, then added, "Come to think of it, O.C. slept atop her pine coffin to keep her from being stolen. I hear tell that's where they found his body when he died April 1, 1950—lying atop her casket."

Definitely a far cry from a Tempur-Pedic mattress.

He lit another smoke.

"I was thirteen when we got the call that he'd passed. My dad, Harold Spain Brooks, was as rough a character there is. About the only good thing he'd done was to take me to Coushatta, Louisiana to bury Uncle Olanda and to bring back Hazel—who was willed to me. That made me like a celebrity 'cause I was the only kid in school who owned a mummy."

As Luther stood to leave, he said, "Some reporter folks say Uncle O.C. left a note telling me to never sell her or show her as some sort of freak, and that he wanted me to donate any profits to charity. Others claim the note said I was to build churches with any proceeds. Well, that just ain't so. We got Hazel, but no note."

"Hold on a sec, Luther. What *did* you do with Hazel?"

He walked over and saddled up on his Gator. Leaning forward, resting his forearms on the steering wheel, he said, "I started showing Hazel at school carnivals, civic groups and such all the way through high school. Even built and added a few rides. When 1958 rolled around, I had a carnival of my own with nine amusements including a small Ferris wheel—and Hazel Farris."

"Did you run everything yourself?"

"Here's the slick thing. My wife and both daughters pitched in—making candied apples, cotton candy, selling tickets, cleaning Hazel."

I pictured his kids wiping down a mummy—definitely not for the faint of heart.

Luther added, "I'd ride my Honda Gold Wing motorcycle back and forth to the bank with the money pouch—carrying a sawed-off shotgun for protection." With that, he fired up the Gator.

"Son," he said, "the day's still early. Let's go make a mess of something."

As he rode away, I heard Luther singing.

"Wasn't that a party . . ."

AFTERWORD

There are moments when separating facts from fiction requires the wisdom of Solomon. I am not he, but I do have a finely tuned baloney meter. That's a byproduct of growing up on the edges of Philly. To survive the big city, circus-like melting pot of high rollers, street vendors, bad actors and squeegee-men, you've gotta sniff out the truth faster than you can say "Liberty Bell."

That's why August 15, 1998 is a red-letter date. That's when I first laid eyes on Hazel Farris, The Outlaw Mummy—yes, in Luther's three-car garage in Franklin, Tennessee.

To be clear, this is a true story.

For two years I befriend, loved, and respected Luther and his personal circus of intriguing characters. He had a deep well of ideas and creativity. His passion for trying his hand at something new was inspiring.

Always tinkering in one of his barns, Luther invented and demonstrated for me the first remote controlled lawnmower ever made. He said, "Even a city slicker can tell that's about as handy as a pocket on a shirt."

Born December 31, 1937, Luther died 63 years later on

January 22, 2000 after a short battle with lung cancer. Puffing through cases of Vantage cigarettes didn't do him any favors.

When I visited Luther in the hospital, he appeared shrunken—not the robust John Wayne figure I first met. He didn't want me to see him like that, but I insisted that he have someone by his side. As strong as he had been, he said, "Bob, I wouldn't wish this chemo on my worst enemy."

Sadly, the treatments didn't work as we hoped and prayed for.

Luther died a few days after my last visit.

On the way to Luther's final resting place, the hearse leading our caravan had to pull over to the side of the road to wait for 30 minutes. Even Luther who, in life, owned and operated his own excavating company, would have laughed at the reason for the delay. Turns out the gravedigger hadn't finished excavating the hole for his casket.

Truth *is* stranger than fiction.

Upon arrival, I helped to carry my friend's casket to the graveside service. I remembered something Luther was fond of saying:

"Guess your train has run out of track."

In Luther's case, based on our afternoon talks about our faith and the Bible, I feel confident his train was Glory Bound.

Today, reflecting back on his life, I'm struck by the way Luther was quick to literally bury things that either wore out, failed, or needed to be put behind him—with one notable exception: Hazel.

Ironically, Luther held onto the one thing that *should* have been buried, probably because Hazel provided him with a sense of identity and significance.

My guess is that we sometimes do the same thing—by holding onto grudges, old wounds, family feuds, and situations which really need to be left behind.

AFTERWORD

Maybe it's time to let 'em go.

I can imagine Luther saying, "But wait, there's more!"

Indeed, Hazel's colorful journey didn't quite end upon Luther's death. Just as O.C. Brooks toured the country and Canada and then passed her down to his nephew Luther, Luther bequeathed Hazel to one of his daughters.

That's when things got a tad complicated. Uninterested in dragging a mummy around—albeit strapped to the roof of her SUV to exhibit at carnivals, she delivered the notorious mummy to Nashville's *Pettus-Owen & Wood Funeral Home* for cremation.

One problem. She didn't have a death certificate.

Reputable crematories frown on reducing a body to ashes without one—even someone who's been dead for 100 years.

That's when the National Geographic Channel caught wind of her dire situation. Professor Ron Beckett, a respiratory therapist and paleoanthropologist, along with Jerry Conlogue, professor of diagnostic imaging, were part-time mummy hunters and co-hosts of *The Mummy Road Show* for National Geographic.

They were dying to investigate the truth about Hazel: Was she, as had been advertised for the last Century, a bona fide mummy—or a fraud? Was she a "genuine human body" or just a made-to-order circus prop to hoodwink people out of a quarter?

Were the carnies right about her history?

Did she shoot the sheriff—and his deputy?

Armed with an X-ray machine and endoscope, the men set out to find the truth. "Hazel is unusual," Conlogue told *The Tennessean* (3/14/02, p.1). "She's one of a group of mummies who were sideshow mummies. We know so much about the

Egyptians, but we know little about sideshow mummies, and this was like opening a window into the past."

Their X-rays confirmed Hazel *was* real, probably in her mid-twenties, and her ring finger did appear to be shot off. They noted exceptionally high levels of arsenic but couldn't conclusively determine that she drank enough to mummify her body. That remains a mystery.

In a startling twist, however, the professors could tell by her internal organs that Hazel most likely had a child—a fact unknown to Luther and O.C. Brooks. They featured Hazel, April 1, 2002, in *The Mummy Road Show* Episode 12: "An Unwanted Mummy."

After a final autopsy, The Outlaw Mummy was finally laid to rest on December 31.

Luther's birthday.

Dedicated to:

Luther Brooks
For welcoming me into your circus

ALSO BY BOB DEMOSS

I'VE SEEN HEAVEN EXCERPT

The first time I saw Heaven I was nine years old.

Don't get me wrong. I didn't have an out-of-body episode. I wasn't in a coma. I didn't drown or get hit by a car and die for several minutes before rejoining this world.

That didn't prevent me from having a visceral experience, one in which I felt as if I were standing at the glittering gates to the Celestial City.

I distinctly recall sitting, feet barely touching the floor, at our kitchen table when I saw Heaven. The aroma of Mom's dinner lingered in the air as my dad began to read the book of Revelation from the Good News for Modern Man.

I was captivated by the description of Jesus with His eyes like "blazing fire" and His face like the "sun shining in all of its brilliance," of the mighty angels with legs like "fiery pillars," and of the New Jerusalem.

I marveled as Dad read: "The wall was made of jasper, and the city itself was made of pure gold, clear as glass. The foundation stones of the city wall were adorned with all kinds of precious stones" (21:18–19). I remember thinking, "Pure gold that you can actually see through? That'd be more amazing than Mom's shiny 24-karat-gold medallion her mom brought her from Greece."

Keep in mind, I was a typical nine-year-old boy who pocketed fools gold, colorful marbles, and the occasional piece of quartz. I had a serious stash of shiny rocks in a shoebox under my bed.

But Dad blew me away when, in addition to the see-through gold, he said this glorious city was covered with a vast collection of gemstones that I'd never heard of before—jewels like sapphire, agate, emerald, onyx, carnelian, beryl, topaz, chalcedony, turquoise, and amethyst.

That had to be way more beautiful than all of the fancy gems in the jewelry case at Sears.

Then Dad read: "The twelve gates were twelve pearls; each gate was made from a single pearl. The street of the city was of pure gold, transparent as glass" (21:21).

Whoa! A single pearl in Heaven was so large, just one was needed to make an entire city gate out of it? I figured that pearl had to be as enormous as our whole house because clearly the gate had to be at least as massive as the one they used in The Wizard of Oz.

Best of all, Dad explained this beautiful city was the place all Christians would be moving to one day to live with Jesus. He called it our "eternal destiny" and our "inheritance" as believers.

Deeply impacted by these descriptions, the second we were dismissed from the dinner table, I dashed down the steps to our playroom. I zoomed to my pile of Flintstones Building Boulders—white interlocking Styrofoam blocks that, much like Legos only a hundred times larger, could be snapped together to make forts, towers, and playhouses—and I got busy building my replica of the New Jerusalem.

Alas, my shabby Flintstone Castle was a far cry from the splendor of the Heavenly City I envisioned. Didn't matter. In my own childlike way, I was engaging with what the Bible taught about Heaven.

As I went to bed, I couldn't get out of my head the I couldn't get out of my head the idea that God would actually pave streets with gold.

Why would He do such an extravagant thing like that? How could anyone afford to do that? For weeks and months I had Heaven constantly on my mind. I'd pepper my parents with all manner of questions, not the least of which was, "Why would anyone not want to go to such a beautiful place like Heaven?"

Over the years, I confess my passion for Heaven dimmed as the clouds, precipitated by the busyness of life, blocked my view. You know the drill. We get so preoccupied raising a family, holding down a job, paying bills, shuttling kids to their activities, repairing stuff . . . attending stuff . . . doing stuff, we forget "to gaze on the beauty of the Lord and to seek him in his temple" (Psalm 27:4 NIV).

How about you? Have you had a childlike "ah ha" moment when you glimpsed Heaven? Was there a time when you realized that God is preparing a place for us more beautiful and glorious than anything we can experience in this life?

Maybe, like me, you've allowed the world to crowd out the wonder and delightful anticipation of our eternal home. Here's the good news. Our forgetfulness "to gaze on the beauty of the Lord" doesn't alter the fact that He continues to prepare a home for His children, one that will exceed our wildest imaginations. Take heart! The day is come when, as Zechariah writes, you and I "will sparkle in his land like jewels in a crown."

THE DEVIL IN PEW NUMBER SEVEN EXCERPT

I ran.

My bare feet pounding the pavement were burning from the sun-baked asphalt. Each contact between flesh and blacktop provoked bursts of pain as if I were stepping on broken glass. The deserted country road, stretching into the horizon, felt as if it were conspiring against me. No matter how hard I pushed myself, the safe place I was desperate to reach eluded me.

Still, I ran.

Had a thousand angry hornets been in pursuit, I couldn't have run any faster. Daddy's instructions had been simple: I had to be a big girl, run down the street as fast as my legs could carry me, and get help. There was nothing complicated about his request. Except for the fact that I'd have to abandon my hiding place under the kitchen table, risk being discovered by the madman down the hall and, in turn, provoke another confrontation. I knew, however, that ignoring Daddy's plea was out of the question.

And so I ran.

Even though Daddy struggled to appear brave, the anguish in his eyes spoke volumes. Splotches of blood stained his shirt just below his right shoulder. The inky-redness was as real as the fear gnawing at the edges of my heart. I wanted to be a big girl for the sake of my daddy. I really did. But the fear and chaos now clouding the air squeezed my lungs until my breathing burned within my chest.

My best intentions to get help were neutralized, at least at first. I remained hunkered down, unable to move, surrounded by the wooden legs of six kitchen chairs. I had no illusions that a flimsy 6'x 4' table would keep me safe, yet I was reluctant to leave what little protection it afforded me.

In that space of indecision, I wondered how I might open the storm door without drawing attention to myself. One squeak from those crusty hinges was sure to announce my departure plans. Closing the door without a bang against the frame was equally important. The stealth of a burglar was needed, only I wasn't the bad guy.

Yet, I ran.

Making no more sound than a leaf falling from a tree, I inched my way out from under the table. I stood and then scanned the room, left to right. I felt watched, although I had no way of knowing for sure whether or not hostile eyes were studying my movements. I inhaled the distinct, yet unfamiliar smell of sulfur lingered in the air; a calling card left behind from the repeated blasts of a gun.

I willed myself to move.

My bare feet padded across the linoleum floor.

I was our family's lifeline; our only connection to the outside world. While I didn't ask to be put in that position, I knew Daddy was depending on me. More than that, Daddy *needed* me to be strong. To act. To do what he was powerless to do. I could see that my daddy, an ex-Navy man, was incapable of the simplest movement. The man whom I loved more than life itself, whose massive arms daily swept me off of my feet while swallowing me with an unmatched tenderness, couldn't raise an arm to shoo a fly.

To see him so helpless frightened me.

Yes, Daddy was depending on *me*. Such knowledge was uncharted territory for my young mind, as foreign and unfamiliar as the dark side of the moon. I didn't have the capacity to comprehend this jarring shift in responsibilities any more than I could explain why anyone would barge into our house with deadly intent that afternoon.

As I turned to leave, Daddy's husky six-foot-three frame remained crumpled on the kitchen floor. I had never seen him so vulnerable. Make no mistake, Daddy was not a wimp. He was a man's man. From the time he was a boy, he excelled at fishing and hunting. I had tasted the venison he'd brought home. When it came to construction, be it painting, building, or remodeling, his hands could manipulate just about any tool with the artistry of an old world craftsman. Having excelled in football in high school and, later in life, having served in the Navy, Daddy knew how to handle himself in any situation.

Except for this one.

Conflicted at the sight of such vulnerability, I didn't want to look at my daddy. Yet my love for him galvanized my resolve. I reached for the storm door handle. Slow and steady, as if disarming a bomb and, allowing myself quick glances backward to monitor the threat level of a sudden ambush, I opened the storm door and stepped outside. With equal care, I nestled the metal door against its frame.

I had to run.

FINDING HOME EXCERPT

There's so much about that night I just don't recall. If pressed for details the next day, I couldn't tell you about the murder weapon. Was the instrument of death a shotgun or a knife? A baseball bat or a club? I don't know. A set of brass knuckles can do real damage, as I've been told. I never learned what went down for certain.

My hunch? A shotgun.

The age and gender of the victim is unknown to me. I've always figured that the deceased hadn't been jumped in the course of a petty theft. My best guess is that the killing was gang related. Perhaps a little payback in the decades-old turf war between the Crips and the Bloods for control of illegal drugs. Or, it might have been a clash between the Latino gang element, the Hell's Angels, or an African-American posse in our racially-mixed neighborhood.

You'll have to forgive me for being sketchy.

I was only eight at the time.

There are two unmistakable facts forever imprinted on my young mind: the yellow chalk line scratched onto the pavement outlining the position where the body fell in the alley. That, and the blood stain. Lot's of it. A brownish-red calling card left behind by the victim for the rain to deal with. My memory of those two images is clear because the murder occurred maybe ten feet outside of my bedroom window . . . a real-life nightmare worse than any dream I'd ever had. And, while I never heard a gun go off, the word on the street was that a shotgun had been used. Talk about inflaming the imagination of a child—no wonder I was afraid of the dark.

We were living in Compton at the time. Yes, *the* Compton—that concrete jungle of southeast Los Angeles popularized by any number of rappers on MTV. Compton was, and still is, a rough place, no question about it. Drive-by shootings, crime, poverty, and vice were a way of life. Speaking of violence, for years Compton had the dubious distinction of being ranked as one of the highest crime cities in all of California.

And now we called Compton *home*.

THE MIND SIEGE PROJECT PROLOGUE

At the edge of the marina, a lone figure sat in his car and checked his watch: 5:53 a.m. He looked up, and, with a squint, his dark eyes focused on the activity below.

He noted that six students had already arrived and were busy lugging their luggage aboard the houseboat. He knew a few of them, at least by name.

They, however, would never forget his.

He grabbed his denim backpack from the seat beside him and, with care, retrieved the seven-inch knife buried beneath a change of clothes. He held the blade up to inspect the tip. The sunlight danced along its razor-sharp edge, as if fearful of the cold steel.

A twisted smirk pierced his face. Would they scream? Would they cry for help? Would they be able to stop him?

No. Of that he was sure.

A voice from some deep, neglected space inside his mind interrupted his thoughts. It whispered: *Don't do it! Do you really think you're gonna heal the pain by causing more pain?*

He hesitated.

For a short moment, he shifted his focus from the knife to the early morning sun as it sprayed warm bursts of red color over the surface of the Chesapeake Bay. He spotted a pelican, perched on the well-worn pier next to the houseboat and, as he sat in the stillness, inhaled the steady, warm Atlantic breeze that drifted ashore.

Overhead, the clouds that stretched across the sky embraced the dawn like an old friend.

With his left hand he tapped his fingers on the steering wheel.

Was there another way?

Could he turn back the clock and stop what he had set in motion? A wave of doubt washed over him. Maybe he could confide in someone. But who? Not his folks. No way. Then who?

And if he managed to find someone, would they understand his feelings—or have him arrested and sent to a juvenile detention facility?

The alarm on his wristwatch yanked him back to the present. Six o'clock. A minute more and he'd be late.

His pulse quickened as his eyes darted one last time between the students on the dock and the knife in his right hand. He knew once he stepped on the boat, there would be no turning back.

His mind was made up.

The houseboat would be the place.

This is how he would be remembered.

He hid the dagger at the bottom of his bag, cut off the engine, got out of his car, and joined the others at the boat.

ALL THE RAVE PROLOGUE

It was 10:33 P.M. Friday night. A seventeen-year-old girl lay curled in the fetal position on the second level of an abandoned warehouse in downtown Philadelphia. Though her eyes were slammed shut, in her mind she could see herself hovering, phantom-like, above her body.

The dark, rat-infested room where she lay crumpled on the floor spun out of control to the pulsating sounds of music she could hardly miss, yet couldn't fully hear. A high-pitched frequency, like a carpenter bee looking for a place to drill, whirled in her right ear. She wanted to swat away the source of this annoyance, but her right arm remained unresponsive. Her legs felt numb, and she discovered that they, too, refused to respond when commanded to move.

Her throat was dry—yet somehow was as tacky as flypaper. She tried to swallow but was incapable of that simple task.

Her lungs, attempting to pull in the thick night air through her pierced nose, were greeted by a nasty mix of fumes and dust. She longed for just one full, clean breath of fresh air.

She struggled to fight back the waves of panic. What was happening to her? Why did her guts feel as if they were about to explode? Why was she perspiring when she felt so cold? Why was she remembering something about wearing pixie wings and pink sneakers?

Just then, her tongue reported something was jammed into her mouth. Her teeth clamped down on its rubbery surface and wouldn't let go. With some effort, she forced her mind to focus. Like the headlight of an approaching car on a foggy night, a dim recognition of the object cut a path through the haze in her head.

A pacifier. How odd. She had given up using pacifiers once she turned two years old. Her mother had her toss her "binky" into a creek in the park, a ritual designed as sort of a rite of passage from baby to toddler. Why, then, was a pacifier back in her mouth now?

As she struggled to make sense of the competing sensory input, she was vaguely aware of an acidic bile traveling between her stomach and throat. The bitter, brownish-yellow fluid ejected by her liver, like hot lava pushing its way against the surface, battled for immediate release.

More than anything she wanted to vomit.

Then got her wish.

Her mind raced in slow motion, searching for an explanation. Maybe it was a touch of food poisoning.

No. No. NO!

Look what you've done. Face it. You screwed up, big time. What are you on?

Pot? Meth? Alcohol? She was fairly certain the voice echoing inside her head, though familiar-sounding, wasn't her own.

Or was it? It was so difficult to tell.

Why was the room swirling fast, then slow, then fast again? Was she dying? Or dead? Was this the last stop before hell? She knew she wasn't ready to die. Certainly hadn't planned to die.

She knew she couldn't speak, yet a feeble voice from someplace inside whispered, *Oh God . . . if you're there, I could use a little help right about now. I . . . Jesus, I . . .*

A sharp pain seared her left arm, interrupting her cry for help. The limb, which had been sandwiched between her body and the hardwood floor, throbbed and demanded to be recognized. She remembered something about a needle, a tranquilizer . . .

With a head full of unanswered questions, she passed out—again.

THE LAST DANCE PROLOGUE

It was Tuesday night and the Philadelphia Memorial Public Library closed in fifteen minutes. The array of five iMac Pro computers arranged on a large wooden table sat idle. At precisely 9:45, a man wearing a loose denim jacket with a knapsack in his right hand entered the old, brick library. He passed by the checkout desk, careful to avoid eye contact with the librarian, and then made his way to the computer station at the rear of the facility.

He took his usual spot behind the computer that faced away from public scrutiny. He placed his bag on the floor at his feet. He cracked his knuckles and then logged on to the Internet, thankful that the head librarian refused to install filtering software. He connected to his personal VPN server to mask his digital identity. The glow of the computer screen cast a pale, bluish white light on his unshaven face as he worked.

Seconds later, he opened his knapsack, retrieved an 8-gigabyte USB thumb drive, reached around behind the monitor and jammed it into the port on the back of the computer which—just his luck— had an available port for accessories and peripherals. Within several minute the compressed contents would be uploaded to his website.

As he worked, a voice from the overhead intercom softly informed all patrons to make their final selections and proceed to the checkout. The library would close in seven minutes. He checked his watch. No problem. He needed just four minutes more for the files to complete their upload.

He continued his routine in silence, his fingers dancing across the keyboard with purpose as he updated the Instagram account with several images to tease his followers with an upcoming live streaming event.

The transfer of data from the disk to the web now complete, he initiated a reverse transfer of financial information to the thumb drive. A smile eased across his face as he reviewed the last in a long string of numbers. This is what they had worked so hard for over the last year. All of the risks they had taken were now paying off big time. He read the number again.

One million dollars.

His eyes narrowed as he stared at the number. With his damp left hand he stroked his chin for a long moment before logging off. He removed the thumb drive and placed it in his bag, then retrieved a lint-free washcloth and a small spray bottle from a side pocket. He sprayed a gentle mist of the special solution onto the cloth and then wiped off the keyboard and the body of the computer where he had inserted the drive. Satisfied, he replaced the items in the knapsack.

As he stood to leave, he glanced at the clock on the wall: 9:58. He flung the knapsack over one shoulder and then took his time as he walked past the stacks of reference materials, careful not to touch anything as he departed. When the librarian offered a good night, he managed a grunt—and no eye contact.

Outside the library, he paused to withdraw his vape pen from within his denim jacket. He inhaled deeply, filling his lungs as he lingered at the top of the concrete steps leading to the parking lot. He began to descend the dozen steps, but stopped when his cellphone played a distinct melody. He had specifically assigned this tune to help him identify the caller before he answered it.

Although he half expected the call, his heart still jumped. His nerves always seemed to be on heightened sensitivity during his trips to the library. He took another puff, slipped the pipe into his jacket pocket, then looked around to ensure his conversation wouldn't be heard before answering. "Yo."

"What's the good word?"

He gripped the phone and spoke just above a whisper. "We just hit the magic number: fifty thousand monthly subscribers. Hold on . . ." He looked over his shoulder as two teens left the building. He waited for them to pass. "At twenty bucks a pop that's, what, a million bucks. I'm talking every month. Gotta love it, right?" He could hear a whistle on the other end of the line. "And this is just the beginning."

"You the man," the voice said. "Come see me as soon as you can. Maybe tomorrow, okay?"

"I'll try. Hang in there, bro." That said, he signed off. He stuffed his phone into the front pocket of his jeans and then headed to his vehicle.

BLACK FRIDAY PROLOGUE

He snatched up the handset of his desk phone with his left hand. His right forefinger, with the force of a woodpecker, drilled the illuminated keypad. He pressed the earpiece to the side of his head. Two hundred miles away, a phone rang in Maryland. The forefinger of his right hand thumped against the desktop with impatience as he waited.

A second ring.

His eyes burned a hole into the phone as if he could will the party on the other end to pick up.

The third ring produced an answering machine.

As he listened to the message, displeased by the failure to make direct contact, he blew a hard breath through clenched teeth. The tone sounded. He spoke two words.

"Call me."

He tossed the handset into the cradle with a snap. He checked his gold Rolex and frowned. As far as he was concerned, midnight always seemed to arrive too quickly. He ran impatient fingers over his receding hairline and through his white hair. There was so much to do and so little time left to do it. With a push, he backed his leather chair away from the desk and then swiveled to face a row of crystal bottles arranged on the credenza behind him.

What would it be tonight? Scotch? Rum? Vodka?

As he reached for a glass with his right hand he noticed the tremor was worse this evening. He stretched out both arms in front of him, keeping his palms down. He commanded his hands to be steady. A friend had suggested the maneuver as a way to maintain control. He thought the whole exercise was stupid but tried it anyway.

It didn't work.

"Figures," he spat.

His lip curled into a snarl.

He stared at his shaking right hand, mad. Mad and afraid of the implication. The tremor had started as a mild twitch six months ago. Three months later, during surgery, his hand had slipped. He recovered quickly, although he couldn't be sure whether or not he had overcompensated. He was fairly confident nobody had noticed.

Not that it mattered. He was the boss.

He reached once again for a tumbler, and then greedily strangled the neck of a $2,800 bottle of A.H. Hirsch Reserve 16 year old straight bourbon whiskey. He poured it straight up. With a jerk, he tossed the drink against the back of his throat and, just as quickly, poured a second glass. Although the office was quiet now, the voices echoing inside his head refused to be silenced. He closed his bloodshot eyes and leaned his head against the back of his generously padded chair.

Just as his nerves began to settle, his desk phone purred.

He placed the tumbler on the desk, eyes still closed, and reached for the phone.

"Yes?"

"You called," the voice said. "What do you want from me at this hour?"

"I thought you were a professional. I pay you enough, don't I?"

The caller from Maryland didn't immediately respond. He cleared his throat. "A minor set-back, that's all. We'll win on appeal."

"Just tell me this," he said, his eyes now wide open. "How could you let this happen?"

"It's complicated—"

"I pay you to keep . . . *things* . . . uncomplicated," he said, leaning forward. He placed his arms on the desk.

"Fine. I'll take care of it," the voice said. "Like I said, this is just a minor bump in the road. We knew there might be some difficulties making our case. On the bright side, nobody in Philly knows about this."

His forefinger resumed its rapid thump. "That's where you're wrong." He picked up a pink piece of paper from the corner of the desk and studied the name of the person handwritten in the upper left corner. His eyes narrowed. "Does the name Jodi Adams mean anything to you?"

The caller hesitated. "Can't say I've heard of her. Is she an ex-employee? Ex-lover? A lawyer?"

"Worse. A reporter, of sorts."

"I see."

"Why is she snooping around my office?"

"I can honestly say I have no idea."

"Didn't I tell you secrecy is everything?" With a flick, the paper floated to the edge of his desk. "I want you to know I don't like what I'm hearing. Make my problems go away—or we're through working together, have I been clear?"

Before the caller could respond, he hung up.

Visit BobDeMoss.com to learn more.

All books are available from Amazon.com.

Made in the USA
Columbia, SC
07 April 2021